# Heart to Heart

# COMPANION WORKBOOK
# for Nurses

Clare Biedenharn, D.Min., BCC

Copyright © MMXX by Your Listening Partner LLC.

All rights reserved. This book or any portion thereof may not be reproduced or used in any manner whatsoever without the express written permission of the publisher except for the use of brief quotations in a book review.

Printed in the United States of America
First Printing, 2020

ISBN: 978-1-953640-00-0 (paperback)

Page Beyond Press (A Page Beyond LLC)
www.APageBeyond.com

**Ordering Information:**
Special discounts are available on quantity purchases by corporations, associations, and others who purchase directly from the author. Contact *drclare@yourlisteningpartner.com* for details.

# Table of Contents

Introduction ..................................................................................................... 5

Chapter 1: It All Begins with a Question ........................................................ 7

Chapter 2: The Bottom Line ............................................................................ 13

Chapter 3: Spiritual Care as Practice ............................................................. 17

Chapter 4: "Hospitality ................................................................................... 25

Chapter 5: Practice as an Art .......................................................................... 29

Chapter 6: Bringing It Back Around ............................................................... 35

Chapter 7: It's Pretty Basic .............................................................................. 39

Chapter 8: Down the Garden Path .................................................................. 43

Chapter 9: The Model ...................................................................................... 47

Chapter 10: Steppingstones ............................................................................ 53

Chapter 11: Riding the Sea Change ............................................................... 57

Self-Care Tips for Medical Personnel by Karen Kidd Lovett, M.Div ............ 61

About the Author, Dr. Clare Biedenharn ........................................................ 63

# Introduction

Thank you for accepting this invitation to dive a little deeper with concepts and practices introduced in the book Heart to Heart: Spiritual Care through Deep Listening.

In a building, the foyer or waiting room provide a place to stop and shift your mind from finding a parking place to preparing to take your clothes off in the examination room. In the church that back area, the nave, acts the same way as it captures our everyday noisy energy and prepares us to step into the quiet worship space.

Just like those in between liminal spaces that hold us during transitions, this workbook is another type of special place. Here you are invited to reflect and react to what speaks to you in Heart to Heart. Deep listening leads to deep connection. Deep connection can lead to transformation for you personally and your patient in that sacred space called 'the bedside.'

This interactive workbook was created to be a place to physically respond to Heart to Heart: Spiritual Care through Deep Listening.

This workbook provides a place where you can think and write and maybe find a new way to approach your nursing practice. I hope you enjoy it as you remember those parts of the book that especially spoke to you.

From my heart to yours-

Clare

Dr. Clare Biedenharn, DMin, BCC

P.S. Please visit my website for a gift from me. It's a downloadable pocket card that features sample questions.

https://YourListeningPartner.com

# Chapter 1:
# It All Begins with a Question

*"If I could give you information of my life, it would be to show how a woman of very ordinary ability has been led by God in strange and unaccustomed paths to do in His service what He has done in her. And if I could tell you all, you would see how God has done it all, and I nothing." —Florence Nightingale*

You ask a million questions a day while providing patient care. "What is your date of birth?" "On a scale of 1-10 how would you rate your pain?"

To get basic information ask a basic question. However, there are other types of questions that can draw out less obvious information that may be helpful. Those open, honest questions open the door to communication on a deeper level. Deep listening leads to deep connection. Deep connection can lead to transformation.

Before we do anything else, let's ask some questions of you. These questions are an invitation to reflect on your personal and professional life.

**How did you come to be a nurse?**

_____
_____
_____
_____
_____
_____
_____
_____

## Do You Have a Dream?

**Where are you now in your profession? Do you have a personal or professional "itch" you need to scratch?**

_____
_____
_____
_____
_____
_____

**What might be keeping you from achieving it or even starting towards it?**

_____
_____
_____
_____
_____
_____

**When you think about your dream, what are you afraid of?**

_____
_____
_____
_____
_____
_____
_____

**When you self-identify as a nurse, can you name your strongest emotion?**

_____
_____
_____
_____
_____
_____

**What's your least favorite part of nursing?**

_____
_____
_____
_____
_____
_____

**For you, what is the best part of being a nurse?**

_____
_____
_____
_____
_____
_____
_____

## ...And You Might Try

**Reflect some more on your story. Remember the faces. Remember your feelings. How do these memories make you feel?**

_____
_____
_____
_____
_____
_____
_____
_____
_____

Keeping track of our feelings can be challenging at the best of times. Journaling can be a way to capture, name and reflect upon your feelings.

**Could you share your nursing story in a journal or with a colleague or a friend?**

_____
_____
_____
_____
_____
_____
_____
_____
_____

**As you look back on your call to nursing, what would you tell that younger, less experienced version of yourself as he/she began on the very first day of the very first job?**

_____
_____
_____
_____
_____
_____
_____
_____

**Consider writing your younger self a letter about that new life in nursing.**

_____
_____
_____
_____
_____
_____
_____
_____
_____
_____
_____
_____
_____
_____
_____

## Just a Thought...

Did you notice that each of the above questions except one was an invitation to go a step further? The question about a "professional itch" could be answered with a 'no' and did not necessarily invite any further response. That closed question could easily have ended the conversation. The other questions encouraged continuing reflection.

# Chapter 2:
# The Bottom Line

*"God spoke to me and called me to His Service. What form this service was to take the voice did not say."* —*Florence Nightingale*

How may I be of service to you? How can I help you to rediscover the motivation to provide consistent, expert care? Care that meets the standards of professional nursing, as well as meeting the institutional standards of your employer? More importantly, I refer to the care that you don't brag about, because it is simply a part of who you are. It is a matter of personal integrity.

Sometimes it is difficult to remain true to that quality while following today's business model of hospital care. The nurse is tasked with a higher ratio of high acuity patients, while managing complicated technical procedures, as well as carrying out the necessary charting. Every day is challenging.

**What can you do for yourself to avoid burnout, fatigue, frustration, and sometimes even a sense of hopelessness?**

_____
_____
_____
_____
_____
_____
_____
_____
_____
_____

**What "feeds" you in your profession? What is it about your work, aside from paying the bills, that calls to you each day?**

_____
_____
_____
_____
_____
_____

## Points to Ponder

**What does service mean to you?**

_____
_____
_____
_____
_____

**If you had to give up everything but one thing about your job, what would that one thing be?**

_____
_____
_____
_____
_____
_____
_____

**Sometimes putting a worry aside for a while can help. Do you have a place to stash your worries?**

_____

_____

_____

_____

_____

_____

**In what way does life intrude and distract you?**

_____

_____

_____

_____

_____

_____

**In what way might busyness be a buffer to prevent authentic engagement with your patients, your coworkers, or your family?**

_____

_____

_____

_____

_____

_____

## ...And You Might Try

As you well know, breath is essential to life. As you go through your day, try noticing your breath. If we're anxious, the breath is often shallow. Stop. Take as deep a breath as you are comfortable with (at least at the beginning). Let it out slowly.

Remember the old saying about doing artificial resuscitation: In with the good air, out with the bad.

Once you notice your breath, you might take it a step further:
- Before you enter the patient's room, stop and take a breath.
- Breathe in on the count of four. Hold for the count of seven.
- Release and count to eight.
- You are clearing out your old energy, burdens, or just plain junk before you enter the room to meet your next patient. You are creating an opening, a clear playing field.

**How was that experience for you?**

_____
_____
_____
_____

## Just a Thought...

The medical world is drastically different from the one you embraced when you began. Establishing your personal parameters ahead of the situation may prepare you if, and when, you feel morally challenged.

# Chapter 3:
# Spiritual Care as Practice

*"How very little can be done under the spirit of fear. I am of certain convinced that the greatest heroes are those who do their duty in the daily grind of domestic affairs whilst the world whirls as a maddening dreidel."* —Florence Nightingale

Religion and spirituality are established as two distinct ideas within the current literature. Religion is described as a corporate faith community that shares a prescribed set of beliefs. Spirituality, on the other hand, refers to seeking the presence of God around you.

What might all disciplines agree upon as basic spiritual care? To begin with, spirituality includes the essential question of what makes us human. This would include respect for the individual, respect for privacy, and other cultural and religious beliefs.

Let's pretend for a minute that you are preceptor to a recent nursing school graduate. **How would you respond to the question, "What IS spiritual care?" Write down your answer.**

_____

_____

_____

_____

_____

_____

_____

_____

# Spiritual Assessment Tools

These are two of the better-known assessment tools. Consider them in two different lights as you read them. How might a patient respond? How might you respond?

## FICA (Puchalski & Ferrell, 2010)

*Faith and Belief:* What is the thread one holds onto as a coping mechanism in stressful situations?

___

*Importance:* How does this belief shape who you are as a person? How important is it to you?

___

*Community:* Are there others around you who share your beliefs? Do you have a faith community for support?

___

*Address in Care:* What does the care team need to do address any concerns the patient may have?

_____

_____

_____

_____

_____

## HOPE (Anandarajah & Hight, 2001)

*Hope:* Where does your hope lie?

_____

_____

_____

_____

_____

_____

*Organized Religion:* Are you a part of a faith community? If you are, is it meaningful to you?

_____

_____

_____

_____

_____

_____

*Personal Spirituality / Practice:* Are there practices you are committed to? Are they meaningful to you?

_____

_____

_____

_____

_____

*Effects:* How does your belief affect your needs? How does it affect end-of-life choices?

_____

_____

_____

_____

_____

These are helpful tools. There is another step, however: application. The same set of acronyms can yield different results based on how they are applied. Assessment can be done

## Points to Ponder

**What does spiritual care mean to you?**

_____

_____

_____

_____

_____

**In what ways might you be providing spiritual care already?**

_____
_____
_____
_____
_____
_____
_____

**What would you change if you could?**

_____
_____
_____
_____
_____
_____

**What part of providing spiritual care is the easiest for you?**

_____
_____
_____
_____
_____
_____
_____

**What part of providing spiritual care is the most difficult for you?**

_____
_____
_____
_____

## ...And You Might Try

What strength could you gain by saying a prayer for your day? It doesn't have to be complicated. Usually, the hardest part is just remembering to give it a try.
- *Please, Lord. Help me through the day.*
- *Please, God, give me the words.*
- *Lord, give me strength.*

If you aren't comfortable with prayer, consider a guided imagery where you draw strength, calm and comfort from higher power.

Remember, prayer need not be lofty in its ambitions. I pray for the person ahead of me in the express line at the grocery who has too many items and then needs a price check. "Please, Lord, help me find some good in this stressful situation."

Prayer can be a specific form, or it can be essentially a conversation with a friend.

**If you were to say a little prayer, what might it sound like?**

_____
_____
_____
_____

## Just a Thought...

The Joint Commission requires a spiritual assessment of each patient. Often the assessment is essentially asking for a declaration of a particular faith or if the patient wants to see a chaplain.

Many nurses are uncomfortable with the topic of spiritual care. While there are myriad reasons that interfere with providing care, one of the greatest ones noted by nurses is lack of training.

Providing spiritual care in a hospital setting is challenging within the healthcare vocabulary. It is not quantifiable or specific and it may not be a service the nurse is comfortable providing. Learning new tools may provide a framework that can assist you.

# Chapter 4:
# "Hospitality

*"To be a fellow worker with God is the highest aspiration of which we can conceive man capable."* —Florence Nightingale

The hospital setting creates many opportunities to stand as God's presence, particularly in difficult situations. In the lingo of chaplains, *ministry of presence* means to be present and engaged as a form of service for God. This is a form of hospitality that is not limited to fixing drinks and bringing out the snacks.

Intentional, engaged listening is a form of presence. You may not feel comfortable to refer to what you do as ministry but listening in a special way can open the door to the presence of a Higher Power, or whatever you may choose to call it.

In *Heart to Heart*, the story of listening to Lester, the man who came to talk with me, provided an example of how there are moments in a conversation that, if we choose to be open, can lead to extraordinary interactions with another.

When I stepped fully into that moment of caring, he told me that he had been diagnosed with a brain tumor. He came to the church because he was scared. He was asking us to help him die. At that most vulnerable moment I was faced with a choice.

**What would you have said or done?**

_____
_____
_____
_____
_____
_____

# Points to Ponder

You may be more of a partner with God than you realize. Consider how might you act in the following situations.

***Action:*** As you look over a new patient's chart, you notice that the drug dose as written could be taken one of two ways. Do you take the directive at face value, or do you investigate until you are satisfied with the answer?

_____
_____
_____
_____
_____
_____

***Vernacular:*** You are present as the doctor gives test results to the patient. No family is present. The doctor quickly leaves, and you sense that the patient doesn't have a full understanding of what was just said. Do you leave the patient without explaining what the doctor said, or do you translate by putting the information in language that they can understand?

_____
_____
_____
_____
_____
_____
_____

*Heart:* The patient in Room 14 is dying, and no family is present. How does your heart, your sense of compassion, respond as you provide care? Does it affect the patient's care?

___

## ...And You Might Try

If you have the time, think about your day as blocks of time defined by activity. Some blocks are longer; others are shorter.

Example 1: A call light goes on, and you go to respond to your patient. His pillow has fallen off the bed. You find the linen cart, go back in to change the pillowcase, and return to your desk. That's one block of time.

Example 2: The family member of a patient comes to the desk. She wasn't in the room when the doctor came, and she has questions. You update her, and she is satisfied. She goes back into the room. That's another block of time.

**Think about your feelings in the two different situations. Are you able to distinguish these as separate units of time? Can you delineate the emotions that may come with each activity? Are your emotions as distinct as the actions involved, or do your feelings about one bleed over into the other?**

## Just a Thought...

Intentional presence takes time and that might be something you don't have much of. But connections big and small can have an inestimable impact on patient care and it can happen without you even knowing.

Asking questions and listening for the response tells the other person that they matter, what they say matters, and that you are willing to engage and see them more than the gall bladder in room 683.

My suggestion is that during orientation every new employee needs to put on a hospital gown and get a wristband. Perhaps that would help them understand just how vulnerable the patient feels.

# Chapter 5:
# Practice as an Art

*"Apprehension, uncertainty, waiting, expectation, fear of surprise, do a patient more harm than any exertion. Remember he is face-to-face with enemy all the time." — Florence Nightingale*

## Handling Your Energy

What energy you bring into the room is important for your patient as well as others around you. Imagine someone says or does something hurtful to you, just as you enter a patient's room. Maybe it was a snide comment, or perhaps somebody just rolled their eyes to imply you did something stupid. The very natural tendency is to react. Often, we hold that reaction in and let it eat at us all day long.

If you don't clear out that anger, frustration, or hurt, you carry it like a cloud that may not be physically visible but that can be perceived in every possible way. Like the *Peanuts* character Pig Pen, who walked around in a cloud of dust, you walk around with a muddled energy for the rest of the day. That is, if you let it cling to you that way.

After you leave work, who's going to bear the brunt of your energy? The cashier at the grocery store? The person who breaks into your lane? Your significant other? Your children? They may all catch the energy you lob their way!

Instead, shake it off. Take a deep breath, and imagine your negative feelings dripping out of your fingertips and dropping to the earth where they can be absorbed and transmuted into something positive. Physically stretch and let your body let go of what you are carrying wadded up in your muscles.

Communication is so much deeper than merely listening. The very energy that you carry with you conveys a message that doesn't need words. Good energy can open a door.

**Have you ever had a conversation with a patient that you felt was somehow "special"? If so, what do you attribute it to?**

_____
_____
_____
_____
_____
_____
_____

**Have you ever felt that your work involves something bigger than just yourself or the tasks that you do?**

_____
_____
_____
_____
_____
_____

**Have you ever had a spiritual experience and discounted it?**

_____
_____
_____
_____
_____
_____
_____

In that special time, you stood in the presence of what is often referred to as the Inner Teacher or the Soul. It is in those times of deep connection that Truth can find Its voice.

## Points to Ponder

Listening is different from hearing
- Hearing is a physical response by your ear to stimuli
- Listening brings meaning to those sounds through mind and heart

What does this mean for nurses and their life's work? ("Don't ask me to do anything else!") In the clinical setting, you are:
- Privy to the most intimate moments of life
- On the front line of patient care
- A symbol of trust

We often hear what we expect to hear. Our personal filter is shaped by experience, and our expectations can affect what we actually hear.

**Can you think of a time when your expectations clouded your reality?**

_____
_____
_____
_____
_____
_____
_____
_____
_____

## ...And You Might Try

You are busy, right? What are you supposed to do with this?
- Realize the possibility that you may connect with others as they truly are, their Souls.
- Slow down a minute. Say a silent prayer if you are so inclined and know that the ground where souls meet is holy ground.
- Remember your call to the work you do and know that you are part of a greater good.

**How will you apply what you're learning?**

## Just a Thought....

Communication is multi-level. We hear not just with our ears but with all of our senses.

Another way we communicate is with the energy that we carry with us and that we pass back and forth during conversation. In *Heart to Heart,* I shared how my grouchy dog Banjo sensed the healing presence of my friend the nurse and allowed her to examine and bandage her sore paw. The diagnosed chronic wound healed in three days once "Banjo's nurse," wrapped the wound. No words were exchanged but Banjo knew a healer when she saw one and her wound healed with that support.

# Chapter 6:
# Bringing It Back Around

*"Nursing is an art: It is one of the fine arts: I almost said the finest of fine arts." —*
*Florence Nightingale*

Practical wisdom is that which is gleaned from personal experience. Experience shapes wisdom as we reflect on actions and reactions that rise from it. As we do, we assign value. Practical wisdom is gained through the process of weighing those observations.

However, there is more. There is that inexplicable wisdom that lies within each of use. Sometimes it speaks to us through our intuition or through "just a feeling." Our rational minds cannot explain it because it is not be seen or heard or carefully placed in a neat file cabinet.

This Wisdom comes from the wise part within each of us. Some call it the Soul or Inner Teacher. Some faiths call this presence God. As described by the Society of Friends or Quaker tradition Wisdom lies within each of us and is ever present to guide us. Humans have free will so Wisdom will not step in uninvited.

Accessing this Wisdom is the basis of a simple and organic listening method used by the Quakers as a discernment process. The method has been used in business, education and healthcare throughout the world.

Wisdom needs an invitation and that can be as simple as asking a question.. A closed question closes the door with a yes or no response. An open question is an invitation that says, "please come in."

An open, honest question is one:
1. To which the answer is not already known by you.
2. That does not lead. A leading question hints at the answer that you expect or want to hear. For example, "Did you go to counseling for that?"
3. That is neutral. "How did that make you feel?" A neutral question leaves room for the individual to respond in any way. There are no inherent expectations.

## Points to Ponder

**Have you ever considered how your personal view of spirituality might affect your patient assessment?**

_____
_____
_____
_____
_____

**We introduced these ideas in Chapter 4. Do any of the three models below speak to you more than the others?**
- Theology in the Vernacular, or everyday speech or presence
- Theology in Action, or taking up a cause you believe in
- Theology of the Heart, or feeling moved to act on the behalf of another

_____
_____
_____
_____
_____

## ...And You Might Try

Practice using open-ended, honest questions. Here are some examples:
- How did that make you feel?
- Why do you think that happened?
- What does that mean?
- How did you think it would turn out?
- What did you mean by that?
- How did that work for you?
- Would you care to tell me more?

**What open-ended, honest questions are you most comfortable using?**

_____

_____

_____

_____

_____

## Just a Thought...

When one of the study participants asked if she had found the listening model useful, she said, "I've become more aware and I sense that sometimes the Holy Spirit gives me the right words for that patient. Especially this last patient who wasn't exactly spiritual or religious. I especially felt it there." (Participant #14)

The nurse listened to her Inner Wisdom, or as she referred to it the Holy Spirit. Wisdom provides all that we need. What it needs from us is an invitation.

# Chapter 7:
# It's Pretty Basic

*"So never lose an opportunity of urging a practical beginning, however small, for it is wonderful how often in such matters the mustard-seed germinates and roots itself."* — *Florence Nightingale*

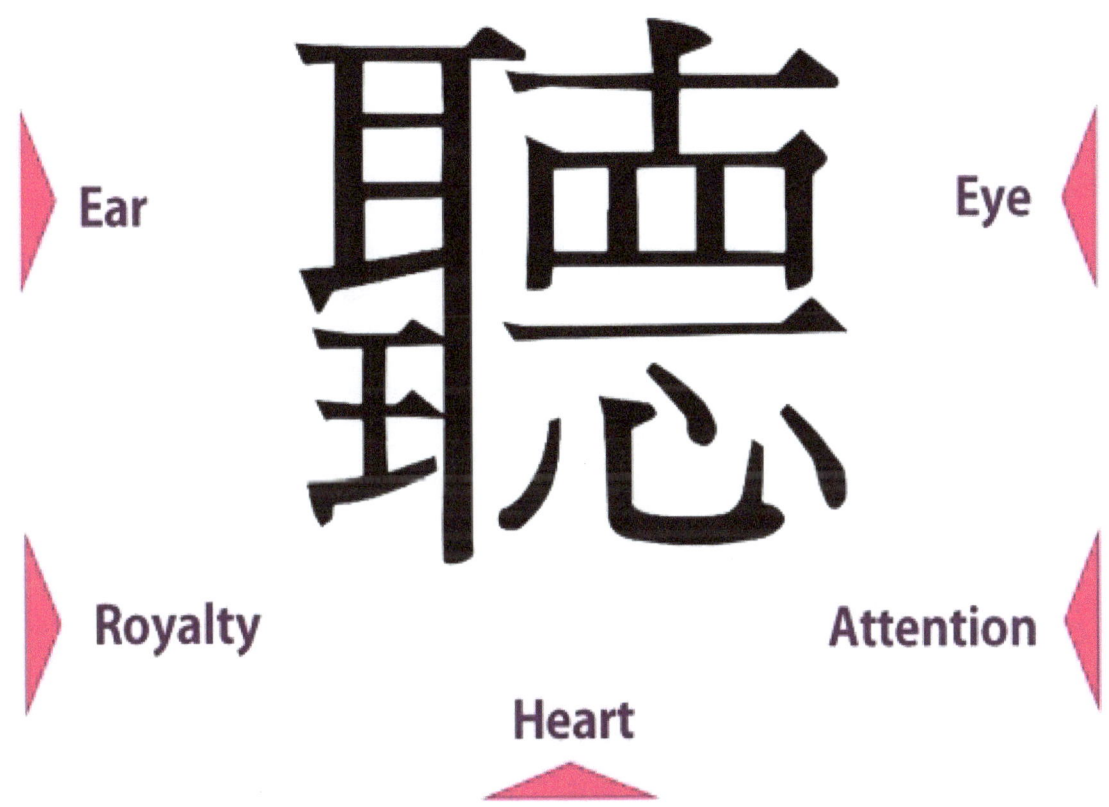

The Chinese symbol for active listening illustrates that in intentional listening we listen on multi-levels

# Where to Start?

A question is an invitation to listen. Communication on every level is the cornerstone of listening. As you assess a patient, what is it you are doing?

_____
_____
_____
_____
_____
_____
_____

As you are running down your checklist, you are asking questions of your patient, but you are also asking questions of yourself. Your questions show the patient that you want to hear what they have to say. When a patient asks a question, treat it as an invitation to step into their life.

# Living with Intention

Remembering to listen intentionally is the key. Is there possibly a trigger to help you remember? What is something you do on a regular basis that could remind you remember to listen more intently? Little gestures or reminders can help.

Two small steps can make a big difference.
- Refresh with a breath, and
- Reset with an intention to be more present with the patient, family member, or staff person

Take a breath and set your intention. To be intentional means to fully connect or to engage.

## Points to Ponder

As you are assessing the patient, they and their family are assessing you. They are asking themselves, "Is this somebody I can trust?"

Intentional nursing is about compassionate care and that includes the art of listening. This is listening in a NEW WAY. Remember: the Ting's the thing!

## ...And You Might Try

Remember to remember. Intention shows your willingness to engage.

Before you enter a room:
- Take a breath
- Set your intention
- Prepare to engage

## Just a Thought...

Intentional listening enriches the patient's perception of care. When the patient is satisfied, it promotes healing and makes the job of nursing more enjoyable.

In addition, sixty-four percent of the questions that appear on the HCAHPS post discharge patient satisfaction survey are directly tied to communication. When the patient is satisfied then it can affect the bottom financial line of the hospital since survey scores are included in the formula to determine reimbursement by Medicare.

"Did your nurse treat you with courtesy and respect?" is question number one on the survey.

"Did your nurse listen to you?" is question number two.

How would your patient respond to the survey?

# Chapter 8:
# Down the Garden Path

*"Were there none who were discontented with what they have, the world would never reach anything better."* —Florence Nightingale

## Listening: Scratch or Dig

The image of the onion is one way to consider the different levels of listening.

### *Think of the questions you ask every day.*
- *Level I - Dry, onion-skin type of question:* "On a scale from one to ten, how would you rate your pain?" This can be a springboard type of question, that can open the door to further communication. Or not. It's up to you to choose.

- *Level II - Next layer of the onion:* The response to that question can draw you to another level. "Has there been a change for you?" This is where Chinese Ting type of listening can be applied, as you listen not just with your ears, but also allowing your eyes to read body language as you begin to give the patient your full attention.
- *Level III - Getting down to the deep, pungent center of the onion:* This level involves listening not just with your ears, eyes, and attention, but also with your heart. It requires responding with open, honest questions such as, "How is that working for you?"

## The Special Space

Remember the last time you came home from work? What is your routine? You opened the door and came in. You put your keys down and maybe took off your shoes before you fully entered the house. There was a physical and emotional transition from the outside world to inside your home, allowing you to relax and enjoy your personal space.

Think about the last time you went to the doctor. You entered the office, signed in, took a chair, and waited. You were not outside the office, and you weren't fully in the examination rooms. You were in an in-between space that is neither here nor there.

In those seemingly calm areas of transition, you have time to catch your breath and center your thoughts before you go on to the next step.

**Take a few moments to identify your liminal spaces and how you might use them in your practice.**

_____
_____
_____
_____
_____

## Points to Ponder

Is it possible that all through the day, your body responds in ways you might not even recognize? Take part of your shift and become aware of your body.
- Someone stands close to you. If it feels good, then you've let down your guard and allowed someone into your space.
- If it does not feel good, then maybe you sense energy that isn't compatible with yours. That's someone invading your personal space. Perhaps it is like that energy vampire Bolte-Taylor describes.

**What does this bring up for you?**

_____
_____
_____
_____
_____
_____
_____
_____
_____
_____

## ...And You Might Try

Notice how many times during the day your body speaks to you.
- Perhaps you hesitate at the door before you enter a patient's room. Suddenly there is heaviness in your chest, and your feet feel glued to the floor
- Your patient says something to you, and you feel a twinge in your heart.

Each of these is a physical reaction to a visceral experience.

## Just a Thought...

So many of us operate on autopilot.

Not long ago the fast-food worker at the drive through window handed me by bag of food. As I placed it on the floor, I noticed the bag from my previous meal. Not only could I not remember what food came in that bag, it took me a minute to remember what kind of hamburger I just ordered

That was my autopilot. What's yours? How do you feel when you realize you're in it?

# Chapter 9:
# The Model

*"[T]he symptoms or the sufferings generally considered to be inevitable and incident to the disease are very often not symptoms of the disease at all, but of something quite different..."* —Florence Nightingale

Expectant listening is a proven and effective model of discernment that has proven itself over the centuries. It is based on the Society of Friends or Quakers' holistic belief in the unity of all persons, at all times, is compatible with the nature of today's healthcare setting.

The belief is that the Spirit, Soul, or Inner Light exists within each of us and is available for inner guidance. Remaining open to this Higher Power as an active participant is an essential element of the model.

## The Quaker Listening Model

The Quaker Listening Model consists of:
- An individual calls together 3 or 4 people to help them discern an answer to a significant problem.
- Only questions specific to the problem may be asked
- They *answer the person's reply with another question*...an open, honest question that keeps the conversation moving forward.
- It is in the interplay of question/ response/ question that the person may access the Inner Wisdom. It may appear as unexpected insight into the problem or a solution they hadn't thought of before

## SAT Acronym

The SAT acronym might help you remember the waiting part of the process:
- Sit indicates your presence.
- Attentively indicates your engagement.
- Trust indicates your belief that the Inner Teacher is present and vitally active in the discernment process.

## How Do You Start?

It begins with intentional use of the listening model.

**Who:** Patients or families who ask you for your advice

**What:** Open, honest questions
Ask question that you don't know the answer to
Don't ask 'yes' or 'no' questions

**Why:** To help person find the truth from within

**When:** To be asked a question is an invitation to help them find their answer

**Where:** Any place that feels safe

Trust the process. Perhaps there isn't a resolution now, but trust that the process is working, whether it is obvious or not. An answer may bubble to the surface later. It is in talking things through that solutions are often found.

**Get ready. If you see yourself a trained listener, you may assume that listening is something you can handle well. Consider this. What would be your response if right now, as you focused on a task, someone interrupted to ask you for your advice?**

_____
_____
_____

What would be your immediate response? Would you hesitate before offering an opinion? Would your mind nimbly run through a thousand solutions as the question hangs in the air?

_____
_____
_____
_____
_____
_____

You may think you know, but often what we think we would do is very different from what we end up doing.

## Points to Ponder

No matter how many or how few are present, there are always enough to form a circle (or a Committee) to help someone grapple with life's big questions.

**Who might you include on your Committee?**

_____
_____
_____
_____
_____

### *Remember:*
- The model is a tool for helping people find their own solutions, not yours.
- The format to use is question-response-question.

## ...And You Might Try

Try practicing your open, honest questions so that you are ready when situations come up. You might experiment as you go about your day.

When a co-worker shares that they watched a movie with their family, ask, "What was the best part about that?"

If your child comes home after a tough day and complains about the amount of homework still to do, ask, "When your friend didn't sit with you at lunch, how did that make you feel?"

When the clerk at the grocery store asks you if you want your bag to be paper or plastic, ask, "What do people usually get?"

That last one is a stretch, I admit. But this is a challenge to "think outside the box." Asking a thoughtful question is a counterpoint to our habitual responses, which often close down a conversation before it begins.

**Jot down some common interactions you have. How might you respond more thoughtfully next time?**

_____
_____
_____
_____
_____
_____
_____
_____
_____

## Just a Thought...

Sometimes you just need a quick answer and that is where a closed question comes into play.

"What is your date of birth?" "Are you fasting?"

Remember the onion? A closed question is like the dry outer skin. It's not connected to the rest of the onion. You get your information and go.

When the conversation requires more attention, then it may take a little time. It is like the rest of the onion. The rings are attached, and one layer leads to another.

"How did that make you feel?" "How did you see it?"

As the person speaks, they are pulling together their thoughts and emotions. In the process they are shaping their story.

The Quaker Listening Model may be a challenge for you because it is not a quick fix. It is organic in nature and results. Like the plants growing in the spring. It can take some time.

# Chapter 10:
# Steppingstones

*"Every nurse must grow. No nurse can stand still. She must go forward, or she will go backward every year." —Florence Nightingale*

The listening model presented in *Heart to Heart* isn't about the nurse solving the patient's problem. It is about helping the patient and loved ones use their own resources, as they make their way on this part of the journey. What if, instead of offering his/her own personal opinion, the nurse tried listening in a different way that is intentional. Deep listening is intentional, non-judgmental, and interactive.

Deep listening can lead to deep connection. Deep connection can lead to transformation for both the patient and the nurse.

Remembering the "why" of your nursing practice can sustain you through the toughest times. It may help to remember that heart resonance that drew you to this work. Perhaps remembering a special patient or a family you helped can refresh you. Each of us has something that keeps us going.

**How would you handle …?**

_____

_____

_____

_____

_____

_____

_____

_____

**Is it possible to come up with a different scenario?**

## Points to Ponder

Is it possible that you can give yourself the same quality of care you give your patients?

What might that include?

## ...And You Might Try

We all tend to focus on what we did wrong. What about if at the end of the day you looked back and noted down everything you did well that day? You may want to start a "small victories this past week" journal. I find this especially helpful in times of high stress.

**Try it now.**

_____

_____

_____

_____

_____

_____

_____

_____

_____

## Just a Thought...

The participants of my study reported that intentional use of the listening model provided three basic outcomes that affect personal nursing practice.
1. Enhanced empathy
2. Increased personal report of spirituality, which mean at times they were aware of the presence of God in their work
3. Improved communication

Intentional use of the model worked for nurses in my study, and it can work for you. The hardest part is remembering to use it. The hardest part is to change your routine.

It's up to you.

# Chapter 11:
# Riding the Sea Change

*"Rather, ten times, die in the surf, heralding the way to a new world, that stand idly on the shore."* —Florence Nightingale

You have been called to be a vital presence in extraordinary times. What you are facing every day as a healthcare provider is far different from the expectations of the job you were called to do. Who could have guessed that today's patient care would be so extraordinarily difficult? Who could have guessed that the work you love would put you at risk personally and possibly for your family? Who could have guessed that even the most basic supplies would be unavailable?

Our resilience lies in how we respond to these changes. Resilience, rebounding in the face of adversity, is the key.

Our response to change determines our survival. It is in how we respond to change that affects how we survive.

Change can be inconvenient and sometimes scary. Consider these questions.

**Are you willing to change? Are you willing to try something new?**

_____

_____

_____

_____

_____

_____

_____

_____

**Will you let it break you, or can you find the good in even the most difficult situations?**

_____
_____
_____
_____

**Are there ways you can challenge yourself and keep from getting bored with your job?**

_____
_____
_____
_____
_____
_____

The work you do is often physically and emotionally difficult.

**Is there someplace where you can go, either physically or mentally, where you feel restored?**

_____
_____
_____
_____
_____
_____

Maybe just a few minutes in the breakroom for a "time out" is all you need to face the next task at hand. Take that moment. Claim it for its value.

Mindfulness is simply being aware. Remembering to be aware is sometimes difficult, especially when you are busy in the middle of the day.

**What simple action could you use to ground yourself intermittently throughout the day?**

_____

_____

_____

_____

## Just a Final Thought...

Deep listening leads to deep connection. Deep listening can also be an expression of compassion. Listening is an easily accessible response to that resonant heart. Compassion calls us to action. Actionable compassion, applying action in response to that tug to the heart, is empowerment.

Every time you encounter a patient, a family member or a co-worker you are faced with choice. You choose how you respond.

Remembering the 'why' of your nursing practice can sustain you through the toughest of times. It may help you remember that heart resonance that drew you to this special profession.

# Self-Care Tips for Medical Personnel
## by Karen Kidd Lovett, M.Div

## 1. Mindset

Simply knowing in your heart of hearts, that you deserve rest and replenishment just as much as those to whom you are giving your all.

Try this exercise: Close your eyes and imagine the person whose love and care you are completely sure of. . . picture them with you and see their care and concern for you and hear their voice saying, " You are precious and deserving of rest, of re-creation, of respite and restoration. Image yourself opening yourself fully to this message of love and care. Breathe deeply and send your stressors and weariness out of your body, mind and spirit as you exhale. It may be helpful to literally make a whooshing sound as you exhale.

## 2. A quick, 60-second break

While washing your hands ( for maybe the 100th time) Breathe in for a count of 5 and exhale for a count of 7. Do this for as long as you are feeling the water on your hands. The awareness of the water also grounds your body and mind; bringing you back to center. There is nothing magic about 5 and 7 other than the magic of focusing on yourself for a minute. Feel free to change the numbers, just make sure they are odd numbers and that the exhalation is larger than the inhalation.

## 3. Ask for help!

Not just at work but at home as well. As a healthcare professional, it is easy to slip into the mindset that you must do it all! If there are others living with you, allow them the gift of helping you. Even small children can carry folded clothes to their room (and feel good about doing so).

## 4. Leave the job at the door!

Easier said than done for many, however, we can train our super plastic brains to compartmentalize very effectively. Develop some ritual when you leave work. Perhaps you image putting all the work worry and stress in a container and put it on an imaginary shelf by the exit door. Try a little Neuro Linguistic Programing trick. As you leave and while using your ritual, create a physical movement to trigger the programming. Perhaps something as simple as touching your chin or collarbone area in a particular manner could be your triggering device.

## 5. Take time to grieve

Take time for your spirit, mind, and body to grieve this hard time and the toll it has taken on millions of people all over the world. For your own wellbeing cry, shout, scream, pound a pillow or . . . you get the idea. This has been, is, and will be—for some time to come—really, really, really hard.

As *critical* as your service to humanity is, unless you come through it still being human, with all the anger, stress, sadness and even sometimes, satisfaction of a job well done, then the virus has claimed you as a victim too!

Peace

Contributed by Karen Kidd Lovett, M.Div

www.aspirelifecoaching.pro

# About the Author, Dr. Clare Biedenharn

Rev. Dr. Clare Biedenharn, author of bestselling *Heart of Heart: Spiritual Care through Deep Listening*, is a board-certified chaplain with over two decades of chaplaincy experience, both in industry and critical care. She was first an industrial chaplain, wearing a hard hat and climbing on oil rigs. From there she transitioned to the bedside in a hospital critical care setting and then to supporting families as they face end-of-life care decisions about organ donation.

"Life-long learner" is a moniker Clare is proud to claim. Her listening study was not only a labor of love, it fulfilled requirements for the Doctor of Ministry in Spiritual Direction (D.Min.) degree from Garrett Theological Seminary in Evanston, Illinois, from which she also holds a M.A. in Spiritual Formation. In addition, she holds an Ed.S. in Adult Learning from the University of Southern Mississippi, with a focus on spirituality in the hospital setting. She is also an ordained minister in the United Methodist Church and served the local church for ten years before entering full-time chaplaincy.

Clare is Board Certified through the Association of Professional Chaplains and holds a Palliative Care Chaplaincy Specialty certificate from California State University Institute for Palliative Care.

To learn more about Clare, or to bring her programs to your organization, visit:

www.YourListeningPartner.com

www.ingramcontent.com/pod-product-compliance
Lightning Source LLC
Chambersburg PA
CBHW061358090426
42743CB00002B/54